HOW DO WE CLASSIFY
MATERIALS?

by Yvonne Pearson

PEBBLE
a capstone imprint

Published by Pebble, an imprint of Capstone.
1710 Roe Crest Drive, North Mankato, Minnesota 56003
capstonepub.com

Library of Congress Cataloging-in-Publication Data is available on the Library of Congress website.
ISBN 9781663970572 (hardcover)
ISBN 9781666324839 (paperback)
ISBN 9781666324846 (ebook pdf)

Summary: Describes the classification of different materials, their properties, and their uses. Includes a hands-on investigation activity.

Image Credits
Capstone Studio: Karon Dubke, 9 (shirt), 21; Shutterstock: Africa Studio, 9 (bag), 23 (bag), AJP, 11, Alis Photo, 9 (brick), 23 (brick), Andrei Shumskiy, 9 (jar), Creativa Images, 26, Dasha Petrenko, 20, Dmitry Galaganov, 18, Dmytro Zinkevych, cover (bottom left), fizkes, 16, Fleckstone, 9 (sticks), frantic00, 25, Iablonskyi Mykola, 9 (bottle), 23 (bottle), Kdonmuang, 15, Line by Line Vectors, 23 (background), Odua Images, 17, Ormalternative, 19, pikselstock, 1, 6, 28, 29, Sergey Mironov, 9 (bowl), sirtravelalot, 9 (rubber bands), soul_studio, cover (middle right), STILLFX, cover (top), Travelpixs, 5, Viktor Gladkov, 27, vystekimages, 12, 13, Wirestock Creators, cover (bottom right)

Editorial Credits
Editor: Erika L. Shores; Designer: Dina Her; Media Researcher: Jo Miller; Production Specialist: Tori Abraham

TABLE OF CONTENTS

Words in **bold** are in the glossary.

FINDING OUT ABOUT MATERIALS

Think about getting ready for school in the morning. You brushed your teeth with a plastic toothbrush. You ate cereal using a metal spoon. You put books into your backpack. Books are made of paper. Your backpack is made of fabric.

All the objects you use every day are made of different materials. Different materials have different characteristics. They could be hard or soft. They could be different colors. In science these are called **properties**.

Different properties make materials useful for different things. Imagine you and your neighbor want to build a birdhouse. What do you need to make it? You need to find the right materials.

First, you need something to make the walls and roof. Then you will need something to hold everything together. And don't forget a tape measure. You'll use it to make sure everything is the right size.

CLASSIFYING MATERIALS

Let's do an investigation about materials. Look at the pictures on page 9. Make **observations**. Why do some objects go together? Are some the same color? Are others a different color?

Draw a line down the middle of a piece of paper. Write *red* on one side. Write *blue* on the other. List objects under the word *red*. List objects under the word *blue*.

You have just grouped the materials by color. It is one of the characteristics they share. This is called **classification**.

paper bag

brick

rubberbands

metal bottle

glass jar

wooden sticks

plastic bowl

cotton T-shirt

Materials with the same properties are grouped together. Color is one characteristic. But you could also put plastic and glass in the same group. These materials are smooth.

To classify materials, you observe their properties. You can observe some properties just by looking at them. For others you may need to touch, pick up, bend, or even break a material.

TRANSPARENT OR OPAQUE

You can use your sense of sight to tell if a material is **transparent** or **opaque**. If something is transparent, you can see through it. It lets light through. Glass is a transparent material. Plastic can be transparent too.

Other materials are opaque.
You cannot see through an opaque
material. Light does not shine through
metal or wood.

HARD OR SOFT

Another way to group materials is by hardness or softness. You can observe this property with your senses. You can feel it. The nails used to make a birdhouse are made of a metal called steel. Steel feels hard when you touch it.

Try tapping your fingers on a keyboard. What did you hear? Now tap your fingers on your shirt sleeve. Does it sound different? The keyboard is hard. It's made of hard materials. Your shirt is made of soft material.

Soft is the opposite of hard. It is also a property you can feel. Think of a pillow. The pillow is made of cotton. It is fluffy and squishes when you put your head on it. The pillow feels soft. You wouldn't want a pillow made of a hard material.

Now think about a sponge. It's soft. It squishes when you hold it in your hand. A sponge can soak up, or absorb water. You wouldn't use a hard brick to clean a dish.

ROUGH OR SMOOTH

Texture is another property you can feel. That is how rough or smooth something is. Think of a nail file. It is made of rough metal. It may also be made of paper. The paper is coated with sand to make it rough.

The opposite of rough is smooth. A plastic cup is smooth. Both paper and a wood desktop are smooth.

FLEXIBLE OR RIGID

You can observe other properties. Is a material **flexible**? This means you can bend it. You can bend leather shoes. You can bend rubber boots.

The opposite of flexible is rigid, or stiff. You can't bend a bike. It is made of metal. It is stiff.

Think of the pictures on page 9. Which objects were made of rigid material? A metal water bottle, a brick, and a jar won't bend. Which objects can you bend? The rubberbands, T-shirt, and paper bag are flexible.

MANY WAYS TO GROUP

Can materials belong to more than one group? Yes! Materials can be classified in several groups because they can have more than one property.

Look at the lists you made of the objects on page 9. Now think about other groupings you can make. A brick can be grouped with a metal water bottle. Both are hard. But the water bottle can be grouped with a paper bag because both are smooth.

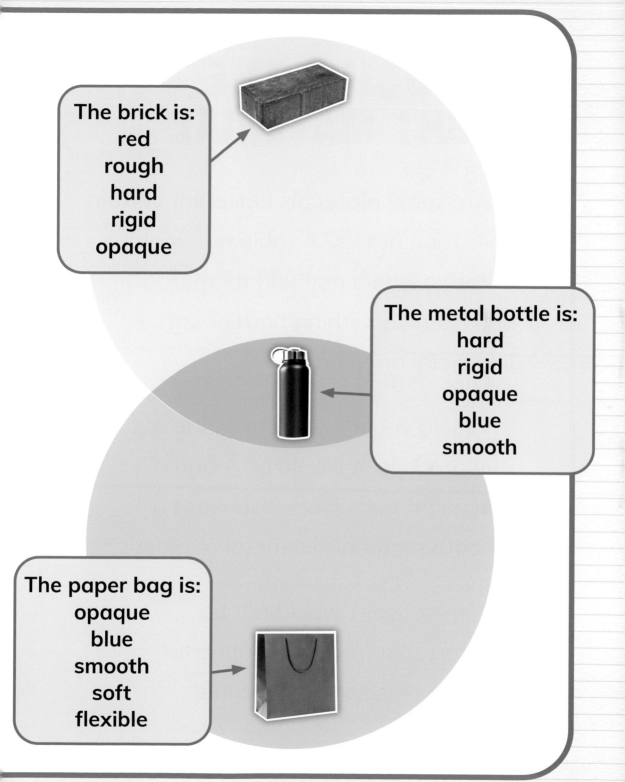

The brick is:
red
rough
hard
rigid
opaque

The metal bottle is:
hard
rigid
opaque
blue
smooth

The paper bag is:
opaque
blue
smooth
soft
flexible

23

CHOOSING THE RIGHT MATERIAL

Are some materials better for certain uses than others? A table made out of fabric would not hold things. You need something hard or stiff, like metal or wood.

Would you make a park slide out of wood? No, it would be rough. You might get slivers. You want a smooth material like metal or plastic.

A metal shirt would not be comfortable. You want fabric for clothing. It is soft and flexible.

Can you use the materials in one
object to make a different object?
Think about a tower made from wood
or plastic blocks. You can take the
tower apart. Then you can use the
same blocks to make a house.

Here is another example. A shirt has fabric and buttons. You could take apart the shirt. Cut the cloth into many shapes. Stitch them together into a heart. Sew on the buttons. You took apart the shirt and used its materials to make art.

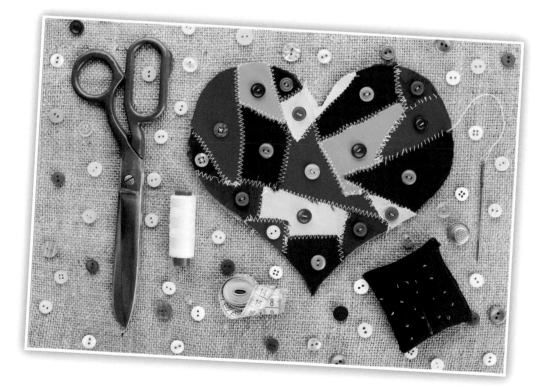

Classifying materials helps us choose the right one for the right use. Think back to the birdhouse. Which materials will you use? You don't want the walls and roof to bend. Wood is a good material for this! Wood is rigid.

Use a metal hammer and nails to hold the pieces together. Metal is hard. When you hammer nails, they don't break.

You need to measure the wood.
A tape measure is thin metal or fabric
that bends. If it were rigid, you couldn't
roll it up again to put it away!

GLOSSARY

classification (kla-suh-fuh-KAY-shun)—the act of arranging into groups of similar things

flexible (FLEK-suh-buhl)—able to bend

observation (ob-zur-VEY-shuhn)—a note about what is seen or noticed

opaque (oh-PAKE)—blocking light

property (PROP-ur-tee)—quality in a material, such as color, hardness, or shape

similar (SI-muh-lur)—having qualities or characteristics in common

texture (TEKS-chur)—the way something feels when you touch it

transparent (transs-PAIR-uhnt)—letting light through

READ MORE

Rector, Rebecca Kraft. *Texture*. New York: Enslow Publishing, 2020.

Rustad, Martha E.H. *Let's Notice Types of Materials*. Minneapolis: Lerner Publications, 2022.

Shea, Therese M. *Properties of Matter: It Matters*. New York: PowerKids Press, 2020.

INTERNET SITES

Britannica Kids: Materials
kids.britannica.com/kids/article/materials/476293

Crash Course Kids: Material World
youtube.com/watch?v=tGfLhPslEjQ

Material Facts for Kids
kids.kiddle.co/Material

INDEX

ABOUT THE AUTHOR

Yvonne Pearson has written 16 books for children, including her picture book *Sadie Braves the Wilderness*. She lives in Minneapolis with her husband but escapes winters in California.